# SPORTING CHAMPIONSHIPS
# Ultimate Fighting

### Blaine Wiseman

**WEIGL PUBLISHERS INC.**
"Creating Inspired Learning"
www.weigl.com

Published by Weigl Publishers Inc.
350 5th Avenue, 59th Floor
New York, NY 10118

Website: www.weigl.com

Library of Congress Cataloging-in-Publication Data available upon request.
Fax 1-866-44-WEIGL for the attention of the Publishing Records department.

ISBN 978-1-61690-130-1 (hard cover)
ISBN 978-1-61690-131-8 (soft cover)

Printed in the United States of America in North Mankato, Minnesota
1 2 3 4 5 6 7 8 9 0  14 13 12 11 10

052010
WEP264000

Weigl acknowledges Getty Images as its primary image supplier for this title.

Project Coordinator
Heather C. Hudak

Design
Terry Paulhus

All of the Internet URLs given in the book were valid at the time of publication.
However, due to the dynamic nature of the Internet, some addresses may have
changed, or sites may have ceased to exist since publication. While the
author and publisher regret any inconvenience this may cause readers,
no responsibility for any such changes can be accepted by either the
author or the publisher.

Every reasonable effort has been made to trace ownership and to obtain
permission to reprint copyright material. The publishers would be pleased
to have any errors or omissions brought to their attention so that they may
be corrected in subsequent printings.

# CONTENTS

# What is the UFC?

The Ultimate Fighting Championship, or UFC, is the world's top mixed martial arts (MMA) competition. It brings together athletes from all over the world to compete against each other, showcasing their fitness and training in a variety of martial arts. Ultimate fighters must be physically and mentally strong in order to rise to the top of the MMA world. Athletes spend years training in order to become UFC champions.

Chuck Liddell won the UFC Light Heavyweight title in 2004.

By **promoting** matches around the world, the UFC has grown in popularity since the early 1990s. It has become a well-known sporting championship. Athletes from disciplines such as boxing, wrestling, karate, tae kwon do, and kickboxing compete against each other to become the ultimate fighter. Millions of fans watch each UFC event, attracted by the skill and power of the athletes.

Georges St. Pierre became UFC Welterweight Champion in 2006.

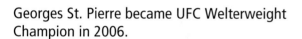

| CHANGES THROUGHOUT THE YEARS | |
|---|---|
| **Past** | **Present** |
| UFC 1, in 1993, sold about 80,000 **pay-per-views**. | In 2006, UFC 66 sold 1,050,000 pay per views. |
| The first 18 UFC events were tournaments, with the champion fighting three times in one day. | Today, each athlete fights only once per event. |

# The Belt

When fighters become UFC champions, they are awarded the championship belt. UFC championship belts are made of leather. Large gold-and-silver plated plaques are attached to the leather. The belt is the ultimate goal for every fighter in the UFC.

# UFC History

In the early 20th century, a Japanese jujitsu master, Mitsuyo Maeda, moved to northern Brazil. He became friends with a local man named Gastao Gracie. Maeda taught the art of jujitsu to Gracie's oldest son, Carlos, who passed his knowledge along to his younger brothers. The brothers practiced jujitsu and combined it with other fighting and **self-defense** techniques. They wanted a way to defend themselves against any style of fighting. Their style became known as Gracie jujitsu, also known as Brazilian jujitsu. In 1925, Carlos and his younger brother, Helio, opened a jujitsu gym in Rio de Janeiro.

In order to attract attention to their business, the Gracie brothers issued the famous "Gracie Challenge" by placing an advertisement in a newspaper. It read, "If you want your arms broken...contact Carlos Gracie at this address." This began a tradition of Gracies facing challengers from all types of martial arts disciplines, including boxing, wrestling, Han Mu Do, kung fu, and karate.

Before he died in 1941, Mitsuyo Maeda had competed in more than 2,000 fights around the world. He is recorded as having lost only two fights. Mitsuyo used his experience to teach young Brazilians and Japanese jujitsu and judo.

The Gracie brothers won match after match, often defeating opponents much larger than themselves. They became heroes in Brazil, and Brazilian jujitsu grew in popularity. Over time, both men had sons who learned the sport and continued the tradition of the Gracie Challenge.

In the 1970s, Helio's son Rorion moved to the United States to teach Brazilian jujitsu. Rorion once again issued the Gracie Challenge, but this time, he offered $100,000 to anyone who could defeat him or one of his brothers. The sport grew in popularity, and in 1993, Rorion, along with his student, Art Davie, organized the Ultimate Fighting Championship. This one-day, eight-man tournament saw Rorion's brother Royce win three matches. He became the first ever UFC champion.

Royce Gracie has taught mixed martial arts to Hollywood actors Jim Carrey and Nicholas Cage.

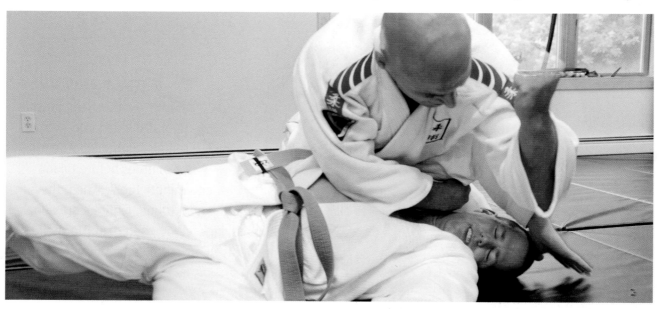

Historians believe jujitsu was started by Buddhist monks in India. Today, it is practiced around the world.

# Rules of the Fight

When the UFC began in 1993, it was known as "no holds-barred" fighting. This means that there were very few rules. Many people found this type of fighting to be too violent, so organizers created more rules through the years. Today, there is a strict set of rules that protect the fighters and make the matches fair.

**1 Weight Classes**

The UFC is divided into five weight classes. Athletes belong to one weight class, depending on their size. Athletes of the same size, or weight class, face each other in fights. Without weight classes, two athletes of very different sizes might face off. This would be an unfair match. Fighters from all disciplines compete against each other in every weight class. This makes the fights fair and safe for each fighter.

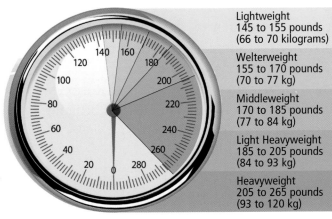

Lightweight
145 to 155 pounds
(66 to 70 kilograms)

Welterweight
155 to 170 pounds
(70 to 77 kg)

Middleweight
170 to 185 pounds
(77 to 84 kg)

Light Heavyweight
185 to 205 pounds
(84 to 93 kg)

Heavyweight
205 to 265 pounds
(93 to 120 kg)

Brock Lesnar won the UFC heavyweight championship in 2008. Lesnar weighs 265 pounds (120 kilograms).

**2 The Fight**

A UFC championship fight is divided into five rounds. Fighters battle for five minutes before taking a one-minute break. Then, they begin the next round. Fighters are allowed to punch, kick, elbow, and **grapple** their opponents in order to win the round. Some moves, such as head-butts, are not allowed during fights.

## **3** Winning

Championship fights can be won by knockout, submission, or decision. In a knockout, a fighter is unable to continue the fight due to injury. Knockouts usually occur from strikes to the head that knock a fighter unconscious. Submissions happen when an athlete gives up fighting. Fighters submit by "tapping out." They use their foot or hand to tap three times on the mat. When a fighter submits, the referee ends the match. A decision happens when the match lasts all five rounds without a knockout or submission. The decision is made by a set of three judges who keep score throughout the match.

Alan Belcher battled Yoshihiro Akiyama during a middleweight fight at UFC 100 in 2009.

# The Referee

UFC referees work hard to get to the highest level of competition. They begin working smaller events and must gain recognition before making it to the UFC. The referee ensures the fighters are following the rules and the match is fair. A referee will order the fighters to stand up if they spend too much time on the ground and can decide if a fighter is too injured to continue.

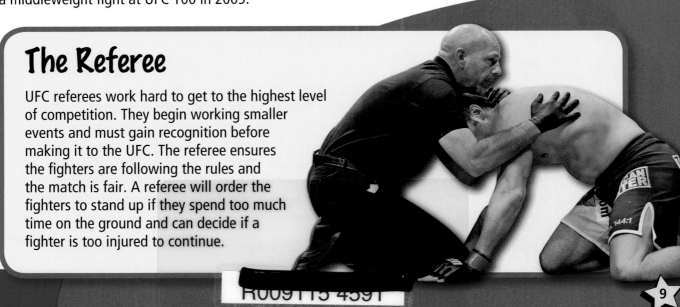

# The Octagon

Each martial art or fighting style uses a different ring for competitions. A boxing ring is square, while a wrestling ring is circular. UFC fights take place inside the octagon. This is an eight-sided, 30-foot (9.1-meter) canvas mat that is encased by a fence. The octagon is unique to UFC competitions. It was developed in 1993 to make the competition fair for all competitors. No UFC competitor has an advantage inside the octagon.

The octagon at the MGM Grand Garden Arena in Las Vegas has been the home to many UFC matches. Drew McFedries and Xavier Foupa-Pokam fought there in 2009.

## Cornermen

Every UFC fighter has cornermen. These are the people chosen by the fighter to help with strategy and to heal wounds. The main cornerman is the trainer, who works with the fighter for months, or even years, before the fight. The trainer teaches the fighter how to win. Between rounds, the cornermen enter the octagon to give the fighter water and stop bleeding by freezing wounds. They also give the fighter tips on how to beat his opponent.

The cage that surrounds the octagon is designed to keep the fighters inside and spectators out. Fighters must stay inside the cage for the entire fight. Between rounds, two gates are opened, allowing the fighters' cornermen to enter the octagon. When the next round begins, the gates are locked, and only the fighters and the referee remain inside.

## The Octagon

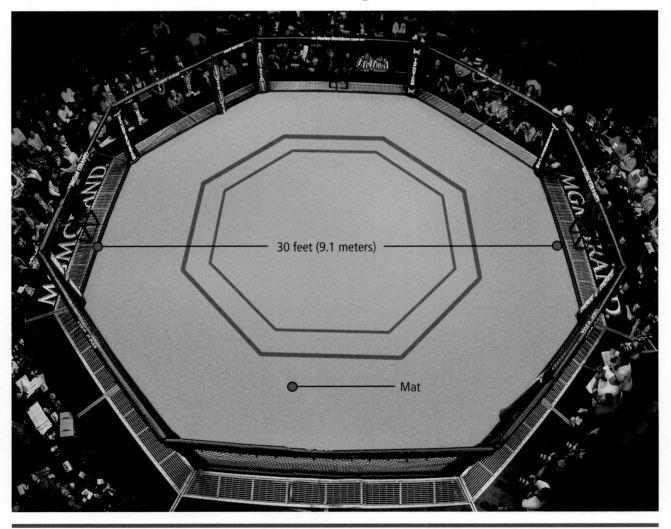

30 feet (9.1 meters)

Mat

UFC fights happen on a mat inside the octagon. A new mat must be made for every event. Mats are sometimes painted with the name of the venue and company logos.

# UFC Equipment

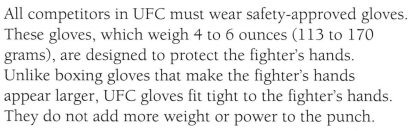

U FC fighters rely on their training, strength, and strategy to defeat their opponents. There is very little equipment used in a mixed martial arts competition. However, training equipment plays a large role in helping fighters prepare for matches.

All competitors in UFC must wear safety-approved gloves. These gloves, which weigh 4 to 6 ounces (113 to 170 grams), are designed to protect the fighter's hands. Unlike boxing gloves that make the fighter's hands appear larger, UFC gloves fit tight to the fighter's hands. They do not add more weight or power to the punch.

Trunks, or shorts, are another piece of equipment UFC fighters wear. Each fighter's trunks are unique. They are decorated with the names and logos of the fighter's **sponsors**. Trunks often are made from stretchy fabric that allows the fighter to move freely.

Gloves

Trunks

**GET CONNECTED**
Find out more about UFC equipment at
**http://ufcstore.seenon. com/index.php?v=ufc_ ufc_equipment.**

Before mixed martial artists are fit for the octagon, they must prepare themselves with strict training. Fighters practice their moves against training partners in an activity called sparring. Athletes try to avoid hurting each other during practice, so sparring requires padding. Sparring partners often wear padded headgear to protect themselves from head injuries.

Fighters practice punches and kicks using special equipment, such as speed bags and heavy bags. These bags often are made from leather or vinyl and are stuffed with soft material, such as sand or rags. Then, they are hung from a stand or the ceiling. The fighter hits the bag to practice striking with speed, power, and accuracy.

Grappling dummies are similar to heavy bags. They sit on the floor and are shaped like a human body. Fighters use these bags to practice grappling and wrestling techniques.

Eric Schafer used his knees in a match against Houston Alexander in 2008. It is important that fighters practice knee strikes because they are powerful.

## Lip Service

Hard hits to the mouth, chin, or jaw can cause tooth and head injuries. To help prevent such injuries, UFC fighters wear a mouthguard. Mouthguards can be made special to fit each fighter's mouth properly. They provide a base of padding that keeps the jaw from hitting the base of the skull upon impact.

# Qualifying to Fight

**M**aking it to the UFC is a challenge for MMA athletes. Unlike other sports, there are no specific measures in place for an athlete to qualify as a UFC fighter. The UFC is a collection of the best MMA fighters in the world. With its growing popularity, more people are competing in MMA events than ever before. This means that there are more events for fighters. However, with more people competing, it is even more difficult for a fighter to stand out from the rest.

Dedication and discipline are keys to achieving any goal, especially in martial arts. The point of martial arts is to learn skills that can help one to defend against others. These skills are not meant to be used for violence. Martial artists use their skills to make peace when it is necessary.

Training is important to mixed martial arts fighters, such as Tito Ortiz (right).

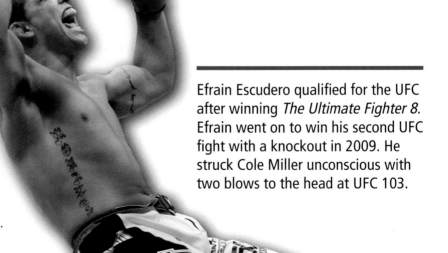

Efrain Escudero qualified for the UFC after winning *The Ultimate Fighter 8*. Efrain went on to win his second UFC fight with a knockout in 2009. He struck Cole Miller unconscious with two blows to the head at UFC 103.

The best way to get into the UFC is to join an MMA gym. These gyms specialize in training mixed martial arts. MMA gyms often are connected to local promoters, who stage events that are similar to the UFC. The gyms choose their best students to participate in local events. A fighter must begin fighting locally to build a reputation. By winning matches and competitions, the fighter will become known in the community. The best MMA fighters in one community are sometimes invited to bigger events around the world. After building an excellent record as a top-quality athlete, a fighter might get a chance to fight in a UFC event.

Martial arts are about making oneself better, both physically and mentally. This should be the goal of all martial artists. Winning competitions and advancing to fight in the UFC are bonuses that only the very best athletes achieve.

Tai chi is a form of martial arts that promotes both physical and mental health. Studying tai chi can help UFC athletes with balance and sparring.

# The Ultimate Fighter

*The Ultimate Fighter* (TUF) is a reality television show created by the UFC. Each season, several athletes who hope to compete in the UFC fight against each other. By the end of the season, only two fighters remain, and the winner is given a contract to fight in the UFC. The show has helped the UFC grow in popularity by displaying the personalities of the athletes and by airing high-action matches on regular TV networks.

# Where They Fight

A crowd of 14,272 watched Brock Lesnar win the UFC heavyweight title at the MGM Garden Arena on November 15, 2008.

U FC events take place in large stadiums and sports-entertainment venues around the world. From Las Vegas hotels to big-city arenas in Tokyo, Japan, the UFC attracts thousands of spectators. They come to watch the power and technical ability of the fighters. As one of the most popular arena-based sports, UFC regularly sells out large stadiums and attracts millions of dollars to the local economy.

**GET CONNECTED**
Learn more about the history of the UFC at **www. completemartialarts.com/ whoswho/ufc/ufchistory.htm**.

Matt Hughes and Matt Serra battled at the MGM Grand during UFC 98 on May 23, 2009.

| UFC Hall of Fame | | | |
|---|---|---|---|
| **Name** | **Date Inducted** | **Fighting Style** | **Accomplishments** |
| Dan Severn | 2005 | wrestling | Only UFC **triple crown** champion |
| Mark Coleman | 2008 | grappling | First UFC heavyweight champion |
| Ken Shamrock | 2003 | wrestling/boxing | First UFC **Superfight** champion |
| Randy Couture | 2006 | wrestling/boxing | Only UFC light heavyweight and heavyweight champion |
| Royce Gracie | 2003 | jujitsu | Champion of first three UFC competitions |
| Chuck Liddell | 2009 | kickboxing | Seven-fight winning streak; all ended in knockout |

Each UFC championship event features thousands of spectators. They purchase tickets to the event, food, drinks, and keepsake souvenirs. In addition to money spent at the actual event, fans who travel to UFC events from out of town pay for hotel rooms, meals, transportation, and other entertainment. Fans who attended UFC 92 at MGM Grand in Las Vegas spent more than $3 million at the event.

The MGM Grand in Las Vegas hosts many sporting and entertainment events each year.

# Mapping UFC Fighters

UFC champions have come from all over the world. Since the first championship was won by Royce Gracie of Brazil, many countries have been represented by the ultimate fighter. This map shows where each champion lives.

**NORTH AMERICA**

**Brock Lesnar**
Fighting out of Minneapolis-St. Paul, Minnesota

**Randy Couture**
Fighting out of Las Vegas, Nevada

**Georges St. Pierre:**
Fighting out of Montreal, Canada

MINNEAPOLIS-ST. PAUL

MONTREAL

SAN LUIS OBISPO

LAS VEGAS

SAN DIEGO

MEMPHIS

**Quinton Jackson**
Fighting out of Irvine, California, by way of Memphis, Tennessee

**PACIFIC OCEAN**

**ATLANTIC OCEAN**

**Ken Shamrock**
Fighting out of San Diego, California

BELEM

**SOUTH AMERICA**

RIO DE JANEIRO

CURITIBA

**Chuck Liddell**
Fighting out of San Luis Obispo, California

**Royce Gracie**
Fighting out of Rio de Janeiro, Brazil

**SOUTHERN OCEAN**

# Legend

Continents

Oceans

Champion's Hometown

621 Miles
0    1,000 Kilometers

N
W    E
S

ARCTIC
OCEAN

**Dan Hardy**
Fighting out of
Nottingham, Great Britain

**Yoshihiro Akiyama**
Fighting out of
Osaka, Japan

ASIA

NOTTINGHAM

EUROPE

ZAGREB

**Igor Pokrajac**
Fighting out of
Zagreb, Croatia

OSAKA

PACIFIC
OCEAN

AFRICA

**Lyoto Machida**
Fighting out of
Belem, Brazil

INDIAN
OCEAN

AUSTRALIA

**Anderson Silva**
Fighting out of
Curitiba, Brazil

# Women and the UFC

In its short history, there have been few women involved with the UFC. There are far more men than women who compete in mixed martial arts. The UFC has never hosted a women's fight, but there are other promoters who feature women's MMA events in the United States and overseas.

Although women have never fought in the UFC, one female broke down barriers by making it inside the octagon. Kim Winslow became the first woman to be inside the octagon during a UFC fight when she refereed a match between Nick Osipczak and Frank Lester in 2009. Winslow earned special attention for opening the gate of the octagon to more women in the future.

Gina Carano defeated Julie Kedzie at an EliteXC event in Mississippi in 2007. EliteXC is a mixed martial arts organization.

**GET CONNECTED**
Learn more about women's MMA at home and around the world by visiting **www. fightergirls.com**.

Learning and practicing MMA is a great way for women to stay in top physical shape and to learn self-defense. Many women practice MMA in gyms, while others compete at local, national, and international events. Much like men who compete in MMA, women must begin by training hard and impressing trainers and event promoters.

Cristiane "Cyborg" Santos won the middleweight championship at a mixed martial arts event in 2009. The event was hosted by an organization called Strikeforce.

# Gina Carano and Cristiane Santos

Gina "Conviction" Carano is well known in the world of MMA. Born in Dallas, Texas, she began her martial arts career by training in Muay Thai kickboxing. Carano won several major Muay Thai events before she switched to MMA. Training with UFC superstar Randy Couture, Carano has lost only one of her fights, compiling a seven to one record. Besides competing in MMA events, Carano is a model and actress. She appears on *American Gladiators* as the gladiator "Crush."

Cristiane "Cyborg" Santos is the top female MMA fighter in the world. Born in Curitiba, Brazil, Santos is the only fighter that has defeated Gina Carano. In October 2009, the Muay Thai and Brazilian jujitsu fighter beat Carano with a knockout. Cyborg overpowered Carano to become the first Strikeforce women's champion. Santos has a record of eight wins and only one loss.

# Historical Highlights

The UFC has seen many amazing and exciting moments. The fitness, speed, and power of the athletes, combined with their desire to win, have made UFC one of the most popular sports in North America. There have been quick knockouts and epic battles to the end.

On November 12, 1993, in Denver, Colorado, the fight featured a huge mismatch in weight. Gerard Gordeau, a kickboxer from Holland, weighed 216 pounds (98 kg). His opponent, Hawai'ian sumo wrestler Teila Tuli, weighed 415 pounds (188 kg). Despite the size difference, Gordeau's speed gave him an advantage. Gordeau kicked Tuli in the head. Tuli tried to recover, but Gordeau followed the kick with a punch so hard that he broke his own hand. The referee determined Tuli could no longer fight.

Martial artist Gerard Gordeau defeated Sumo wrestler Teila Tuli 26 seconds into their fight at the first UFC event.

| UFC Records | | |
|---|---|---|
| **Record** | **Athlete** | **Country of Birth** |
| Most wins (16) | Chuck Liddell<br>Matt Hughes | United States<br>United States |
| Most consecutive wins (10) | Anderson Silva | Brazil |
| Most fights (22) | Chuck Liddell<br>Tito Ortiz | United States<br>United States |
| Most title wins (9) | Matt Hughes<br>Randy Couture | United States<br>United States |

About 775,000 television viewers paid to watch Ken Shamrock and Tito Ortiz fight at UFC 61.

Ken Shamrock and Tito Ortiz are two of the best-known names in UFC. Ortiz and Shamrock first paired off at UFC 40. Despite an injury, Shamrock stepped into the cage with Ortiz. He was defeated by a total knockout.

The main event of UFC 61 in Hollywood, Florida, featured a rematch between Shamrock and Ortiz. Only one minute and 18 seconds into the first round, Ortiz won the match. The referee decided Shamrock had taken too many hits and could no longer defend himself. Shamrock protested the decision, and a rematch was planned.  It would air on regular TV. About 5.7 million viewers watched as, once again, Ortiz ended the fight early, only two minutes and 23 seconds into the first round. Only one UFC event has attracted more television viewers since.

UFC 69 saw a great upset in sports history. As the winner of Season 4 of *The Ultimate Fighter*, Matt Serra was given a title match against champion, Georges St. Pierre in Houston, Texas. St. Pierre was heavily favored to win the fight, and Serra seemed to enjoy his role as underdog. It took only three minutes and 23 seconds for Serra to take St. Pierre to the mat and win the fight. The outcome was shocking to UFC fans.

# LEGENDS
## and Current Stars

## Royce Gracie

### Ken Shamrock

Ken Shamrock is known as "The World's Most Dangerous Man." He earned this nickname with his incredible strength and skill in mixed martial arts. Living on the streets when he was only 10 years old, Shamrock learned to box and wrestle at a group home when he was 13. Eventually, Ken went to wrestle in Japan, where he became a superstar. He returned to the United States and opened the Lion's Den in Lodi, California. There, he trains people in MMA. Shamrock is well known for his time spent in World Championship Wrestling but is best known as a four-time UFC champion.

### Royce Gracie

Royce Gracie comes from the most influential family in mixed martial arts. His brother, Rorion, who started the UFC, chose Royce to represent the Gracie family at UFC 1. Rorion believed that Royce, weighing under 180 pounds (81.6 kg), would show the world how Gracie jujitsu could defeat brute strength and size. Royce went on to win UFC 1 and UFC 2 but lost UFC 3. He won again at UFC 4, before **drawing** with Ken Shamrock at UFC 5 in 1995. In 2006, Gracie returned to UFC. He met Matt Hughes and lost in the first round. Royce remains the greatest legend in UFC history.

### Ken Shamrock

## Chuck Liddell

## Anderson Silva

Anderson Silva grew up in Curitiba, Brazil. He began learning martial arts by watching other children practice Brazilian jujitsu. Eventually, Silva earned money to pay for tae kwon do lessons. Later, he studied **capoeira**. By the time he was 16, Silva was training in Muay Thai. In his first UFC fight, Silva knocked out Chris Leben in only 49 seconds. He won the UFC middleweight championship at UFC 64 and has defended it six times. Silva is known as "the Spider" because of his long arms and legs.

## Chuck Liddell

When he was 12 years old, Chuck Liddell saw a television show called *Kung-Fu Theater* and was inspired to learn karate. He was a dedicated student who also mastered the arts of kickboxing, wrestling, and Brazilian jujitsu. Although Liddell had won several national kickboxing tournaments, he knew that it would be difficult to make money as a fighter. Instead, he went to university. Liddell earned a degree in accounting from California Polytechnic State University while wrestling for the school team. He became the UFC light heavyweight champion at UFC 52, and defended the title five times.

## Anderson Silva

# Famous Firsts

At UFC 5 in April, 1995, Royce Gracie met Ken Shamrock in the octagon for a match called the Superfight. It was a head-to-head battle for the championship. In the early days of UFC, there were no rounds or time limits. When the fighters went to the ground, they stayed there. With very little action for more than 30 minutes, the fight was ended and called a draw. About 260,000 pay-per-view customers were disappointed with the result. Their upset called for rule changes that made the competition more exciting. They added rounds and judges, among other changes.

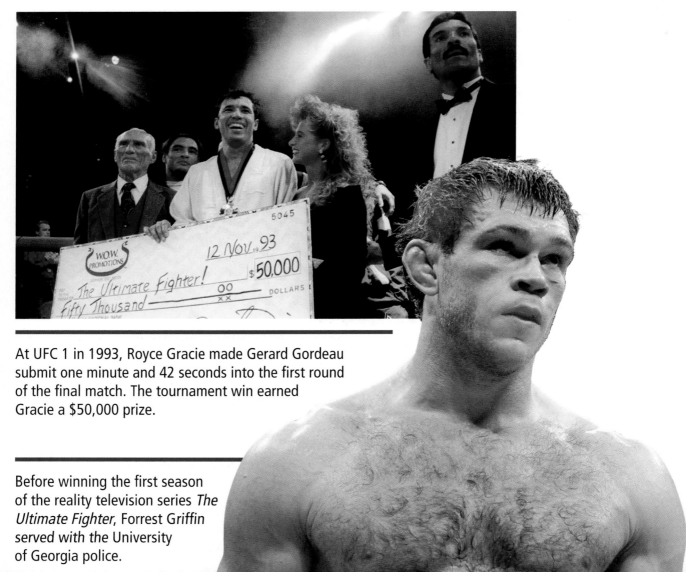

At UFC 1 in 1993, Royce Gracie made Gerard Gordeau submit one minute and 42 seconds into the first round of the final match. The tournament win earned Gracie a $50,000 prize.

Before winning the first season of the reality television series *The Ultimate Fighter*, Forrest Griffin served with the University of Georgia police.

B.J. Penn is the first American-born winner of the World Brazilian jujitsu Championship.

*The Ultimate Fighter 1*, in 2005, ended with one of the greatest matches in UFC history. Forrest Griffin and Stephen Bonnar battled for three electrifying rounds, knowing that only one of them would be given a UFC contract. In the end, it was Griffin who won by decision. UFC President, Dana White called the match "the most important fight in UFC history." As fans in Sacramento, California cheered, White surprised everyone by awarding contracts to both fighters.

New Year's Eve 2008 was the first time two current UFC champions met in the octagon. Promoted as the biggest fight in UFC history, lightweight champion B.J. Penn faced welterweight champion Georges St. Pierre for the welterweight championship. Penn had the chance to become the first fighter with two championship belts at the same time. The fight lasted until the fourth round when Penn's corner threw in the towel, surrendering to St. Pierre.

# The First UFC

UFC 1 was held on November 17, 1993, in Denver, Colorado. It was a one-day tournament featuring eight fighters who competed head-to-head for the championship. The day's first match was between Gerard Gordeau and Teila Tuli, followed by Kevin Rosier who knocked out Zane Frazier. The tournament also featured Ken Shamrock, who later become one of the biggest stars in UFC history. Shamrock was defeated in the semifinal by Royce Gracie, who went on to beat Gordeau in the final to become the first Ultimate Fighting Champion.

# The Rise of the UFC

## 1925

Carlos and Helio Gracie open a jujitsu academy in Rio de Janeiro, Brazil, and issue the Gracie Challenge.

## 1993

Rorion Gracie and Art Davie start the UFC.

## 1997

UFC fighter Tank Abbott, announcer Bruce Buffer, and referee Big John McCarthy guest star on an episode of the TV show *Friends*.

## 1999

UFC rules change to include five-minute rounds and a 10-point system for judging that is based on boxing.

## 2000

The company that owns the UFC fails, and it is bought by Zuffa, Inc.

## 2001

The rules of UFC are changed to make the sport safer and to showcase skill rather than violence.

## 2003

Ken Shamrock and Royce Gracie are the first two inductees into the UFC Hall of Fame.

## 2005

*The Ultimate Fighter*, a reality TV show, airs for the first time.

## 2006

In December, UFC light-heavyweight champion Chuck Liddell fights former champion Tito Ortiz. The fight receives more than one million pay-per-view buys.

## 2008

About 21,000 people watch UFC 83 at the Bell Centre in Montreal, Canada. It is the largest crowd ever to watch an MMA event in North America.

## 2009

Brock Lesnar is the UFC heavyweight champion.

## 2007

Zuffa, Inc. buys Pride Fighting Championship, a Japanese MMA league similar to UFC.

## QUICK FACTS

- Mark Coleman won UFC 11 without having to fight in the final round. His opponent was in the hospital.

- Zuffa Inc. bought the UFC for $2 million. Today, it is worth more than $700 million.

- Originally, UFC promoters wanted to include an electric fence and alligators around the octagon. They decided it was too dangerous.

# Test Your Knowledge

**1** Who was the first UFC champion?

**2** What trophy is the UFC champion awarded?

**3** Where do UFC fights take place?

**4** What are the only pieces of equipment worn by UFC fighters today?

**5** What is the name of the UFC reality TV show?

**6** Who won the UFC lightweight belt at UFC 101?

**7** Who was the first female referee in the UFC?

**8** Who holds the record for most consecutive UFC victories?

**9** What is Ken Shamrock's nickname?

**10** Who won the first season of The *Ultimate Fighter*?

**ANSWERS:** 1) Royce Gracie 2) A championship belt 3) Inside the octagon 4) Gloves, mouthguard, and trunks 5) *The Ultimate Fighter* 6) B.J. Penn 7) Kim Winslow 8) Anderson Silva 9) The World's Most Dangerous Man 10) Forrest Griffin

# Further Research

There is more information about the UFC available on websites and in books. To learn more about the UFC, visit your library, or look online.

## Books to Read

Search your library for books about the UFC. On your library's computer, type in a keyword. The computer will help find information you are looking for. You can also ask a librarian for help.

## Online Sites

You can learn much more about MMA and the UFC at www.ufc.com

Check out *The Ultimate Fighter* at www.spike.com/show/22307

Find an MMA gym by visiting www.findmmagym.com

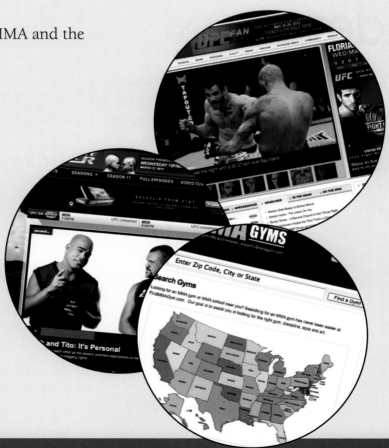

# Glossary

**capoeira:** a martial art that combines music and dance

**drawing:** calling a tie

**grapple:** when two fighters grab each other around the shoulders or waist

**pay-per-views:** the amount of people who pay to watch the UFC on their own television

**promoting:** people who organize an event and bring attention to it through advertising

**self-defense:** protecting oneself from violence or harm

**sponsors:** companies who pay to have their logo shown at a UFC event

**Superfight:** a non-tournament match held in the early days of the UFC

**triple crown:** three different titles in the same organization

# Index